It's Coming Back: *Vengeance Is the Lord's, So, Stop Making Weapons*

by Dr. Marlene Miles

Freshwater Press 2024

freshwaterpress9@gmail.com

ISBN: 978-1-965772-04-1

Paperback Version

Table of Contents

It's Coming Back

Vengeance Is the Lord's, So Stop Creating Evil Weapons

Freshwater

Prayer of Salvation

Lord Jesus, come into my life. I accept You as my Lord and Personal Savior. I believe in my heart that You are the Son of God and that You died and rose from the dead to save me. Thank You, Lord for saving me, in Jesus' Name, Amen.

Two Sides

I get tired of hearing that there are two sides to every story. One of the reasons I tire of it, like most people, I want whomever I am telling my side to, to agree with me. Period.

But they don't always. Sometimes they never. Some friends are friends to simply disagree with you, or to help you see the other side of an issue. We all need balance and to be balanced.

In the scheme of two sides, there is really only one right side; God's side. God is right and we humans can agree with God, or we can be partially right, or completely wrong.

This book explores evil arrows from two sides, the side that sent it, and the side that receives it, gets hit with it, or that it was intended for.

We have to look at both sides of this issue to learn what we must know about the issue of evil arrows. And the other side of the story is about sending evil arrows **back** to the one who dealt it.

It's Coming Back

It is sad that there is so much witchcraft in the world, but that has always been the case, else the Bible wouldn't be riddled with examples and warnings, and solutions regarding it. Of course, this volume is not to or about the people that witchcraft doesn't touch and can't touch--, the perfect and the undefiled. I'm not sure who or where those people are---, the perfect, and the undefiled; but God knows.

Those of old who believed that they were perfect---, the Pharisees, spent so much time trying to get rid of Jesus who was here on mission from God was their focus as Jesus helped people who were sinners and may have been for all we know the victims of witchcraft and occultism. Obviously, Pharisees seem to have had no problems with witchcraft. I say that because there is no historical accounts of them fighting it. But they had problems with Jesus, who stood 100% for the Truth, for Light, and the Kingdom of Heaven. When we see someone who is totally offended by Jesus, they are most often working for, or are in agreement with the other side, the dark side.

Isn't something backward here?

Witchcraft is everywhere. How do I know? It's discussed in the Bible. We may not always see witchcraft, but we can see the signs of it. If we can't see it in ourselves, sometimes that movie is playing right before our eyes and we can see it in a loved one, a friend, an acquaintance, or a co-worker.

We must know the signs of witchcraft attack. If we are ignorant of that, we won't see a thing, know a thing, and may whistle along in life blissfully ignorant and possibly suffering, or mysteriously dead.

Witches work for the guy who comes only to steal, kill **and** destroy, so what do you think patterns of their attacks will look like? Once their evil arrows _hit_, what do you think the terrain of a person's life will look like?

They will be stolen from, killed, and or destroyed. They may even look like David's men from 1 Samuel 22:2.

And every one _that was_ in distress, and every one that _was_ in debt, and every one _that was_ discontented, gathered themselves unto him; and he became a captain over them: and there were with him about four hundred men. (1 Samuel 22:2)

This is what the devil and his evil agents want their victims to look like, if they are even alive, else they'd like them dead. Evil arrows are to make one become broke, busted, and disgusted. There is hope though, if we gather ourselves to the Captain of Our Souls, we can be victorious over the plots and plans of the enemy. But first we must submit to

Christ's leadership and learn how to do battle and become mighty warriors in these spiritual matters.

We will speak primarily of evil arrows in this book, but there are multiple ways of witchcraft attack. Many of these ways fall under the general definition of evil arrows.

An evil arrow is a demonic missile that the enemy shoots into the spiritual realm. Its purpose is to attack people and their destinies. There are two basic categories, those that cause affliction or arrows of death. So, these arrows cause chaos, pain, and tragedy in the lives of their victims. These arrows cause physical, emotional, mental, spiritual harm by their spiritual impact and also by their smell. Evil smell is not in the scope of this book, but look for a book on that subject by Pastor Veronica Muviti. The release date is unknown at this printing.

People can end up in the hospital after receiving spiritual arrows of darkness. Why do you think Emergency Rooms are so busy, whether there is a pandemic going on or not? Evil arrows.

There are two choices if we are being shot at with evil arrows. We can send back evil arrows, or we can suffer, blindly, ignorantly, pridefully. We can pray for spiritual surgery to take them out or we can go to the ER, an emergency clinic or our regular primary care physician in the natural realm. In those places we can just watch medical doctors and other caregivers shake their heads while finding nothing wrong with us. Nothing at all. You just missed a day from work, lost time, lost money in copays and possibly prescription meds and over the counter self-medicating remedies.

Carnal medical doctors can't see a spiritual evil arrow. And by training, even if they can, they are trained not to tell you such a thing. Just the facts--, just the physical facts are all they are allowed to deal with. Most of them are left-brained anyway and do not think spiritually. Therefore, you will be looked at suspiciously, or sadly as if, what is wrong with you by a worldly physician or nurse. All the while your medical practitioner is protecting his or her medical license by not saying anything other than what he is trained to see and say from medical school.

As frustrating as it is to have something wrong with you, to be in pain, or out of sorts, at least that frustration is only for those who receive arrows of affliction. When arrows of death strike, those people may not even be fortunate enough to last long enough to even see a medical doctor. It's lights out, mysteriously and sometimes suddenly.

I'm not your medical practitioner, and I am not diagnosing anything, I am only giving you spiritual information that may help you now or in the future. If you don't need this book, pass it along, or if you do need it, soak it in, and also recommend it to another who may need it.

Evil arrows are sent to steal, kill, destroy, block, hinder, or to confound the intended victim.

When an arrow is fired against a believer one of many scenarios may unfold.

1. It can bounce back, be deflected by the shield of Faith, and go back to the sender. The whole armor of God is very protective.
2. The Shield of Faith is designed to quench fiery darts and I supposed, evil arrows.
3. The Hedge of Fire that may be around you may completely consume that evil arrow or anything else that comes up against you.

4. It can enter in and begin to afflict the victim immediately.

5. It can enter into the person but be programmed to commence devastation at a later date or time. People who feel things moving in their body—that's an evil arrow that is preparing to harm them.

6. It can pass *through* the body, creating a spiritual exposure, an access point for more evil to enter in, or a spiritual injury in the person.

7. It can keep following the person like a cartoon cloud that will only rain on that person. It may remain around a person until opportunity presents.

Evil arrows are possible because of evil altars. If a person is especially hated, or especially targeted, arrows can come from more than one altar, even multiple altars. Those altars could be ancient, old, contemporary, or as recent as yesterday, depending on what sins your ancestors committed and didn't repent of, all the way up to what you may have done and have not repented for.

Always remember because of ancient altars that are still being attended to, you may be suffering. Evil arrows emanate from evil altars that are firing against you and or your bloodline.

No matter how many enemies you have, known or unknown, no matter how many altars, no matter how many arrows, you have a right to command evil arrows to go back to where they came from. If evil arrows are being sent against you, it would be unwise not to send them back, else you will suffer and may even die.

According to Psalm 105:15, *Touch not mine anointed, do my prophet no harm,* we see God's stance on defending ourselves against evil emanations. But if you have not been made aware that an evil arrow has been sent or will be sent against you, you might not do anything. If you don't hear from the Holy Spirit and get into warfare, that arrow may hit. If you don't believe there's such a thing, then keep on living.

Arrows can come from any place at any time. You may be surprised to find out who would do such a thing— sometimes it's folks you know; sometimes it's folks you are related to. It could be from an ancient family altar in a far away country—a distant relative that you never met, never heard of and never did anything to.

It could be a complete stranger, a teen, a novice sending out evil arrows just to see if they hit. It could be some evil human agent on assignment who is in evil covenant with the devil, either on purpose or by mistake, and they must do this or suffer whatever consequences are in their evil covenant if that human doesn't fulfill their end of the evil contract.

For they do not sleep unless they have done evil; And their sleep is taken away unless they make *someone* fall. (Proverbs 4:16 NKJV)

The hunter may be monitoring the person to see what happens to the arrows. They may ordain arrows for a particular person in which case the arrows keep following the person until there is space to attack the person.

You don't need to know who is sending arrows in order to do warfare. As a matter of fact, you might do better not to know. If you know, you might not want to do warfare because you love them so much. Because they are your best friend, or cousin. They could be your mother. It might be better not to know so you can objectively do warfare. If you are a sober mature sort, you might be fine to know who it is. As I have prayed the Lord has shown me faces of who did what.

(Boy, oh boy is this going to surprise a lot of you.)

Know this, if they are sending evil arrows at you, there is no love from them to you, so fight for your destiny and fight for your life. War!

Why Me?

What makes you attackable by evil arrows?

No one is saying that another is *just asking for it*, but evil human agents will look at certain markers as to whether a person is a good candidate to fire evil arrows at, or not. Surely, they have no right to judge you, but they do. This is why *monitoring spirits* are sent, to size you up, spiritually. If you are an easy target or would make a good victim, then they'll proceed. Not only that, they also want to know the best day and the best way to attack their intended victim.

If you sense *monitoring spirits,* then start praying immediately, not just about the *monitoring spirit*, but you have to protect yourself from the onslaught that may be planned against you. Send back evil arrows, even if it is pre-emptive. Ask God if you should launch an offensive against those making the plans. If you are spiritually strong enough, do it yourself. If you need spiritual support to accomplish this, then get it.

The answer to fighting the kingdom of darkness is never to hire someone from the kingdom of darkness to fight for you. Of course, devils fighting devils could be amusing, but Satan cannot cast out Satan.

So, if a *monitoring spirit* reports any of the following things back to their evil human agent, you will look like a sitting duck for evil arrows.

- Lackluster spiritually and dry prayer life.
- In sin, any kind, but especially sexual sin.
- In anger, unforgiveness, bitterness is a breeding ground for demons.

- Fearing, as in Job's words, *greatly fearing* will draw what you fear right to you.
- Doubt and unbelief.
- Not being saved, or just hanging around the edge of salvation--, not fully *in*. Doing the bare minimum, such as adopting or declaring the *I'm a good person philosophy.*
- Using substances such as alcohol and mood and mind-altering drugs make you a good candidate for evil.

While you are temporarily (we hope) not using your faculties, demons of any sort can enter into you and take up residence and use your body.

If someone has the nerve or the assignment to send a curse or evil arrows, at you--, unprovoked and unsolicited **but that evil arrow doesn't alight** – IT IS COMING BACK TO THE SENDER. Automatic or by force, it's coming back.

No curse can alight without a cause. If there is no cause for an evil arrow to hit you, or anyone else for that matter, it just won't. The cause could be an open ancestral door, iniquity from ancestors' or your sin, or defilement on your part.

The *cause* can't be just *because you don't like them*, or they don't like you, although for many witches, many who send out evil arrows, that is *their* cause. Gray collar witches aren't sending out their own arrows; they are also considered to be witches for entering into the agreement <u>with a witch</u> by paying someone to do evil for them.

If it doesn't hit, it is coming back, automatically. If it doesn't hit and the target sends it back; it's coming back. It is coming back against the one who sent it **and** the one who paid the witch to send it.

For the arrow to land, the *cause* has to be either sin in the victim, or other form of defilement. One can be affected by collateral evil arrow damage by being in the wrong place or in association with the sinful or defiled target. That is why if you are walking upright before the Lord, that arrow won't hit; but who is perfect? This is why evil agents of the human variety, and spiritual kind either try to get you to sin, because if you sin, now you are compromised, and their arrows can hit.

Be ye therefore perfect, even as your Father which is in heaven is perfect.
(Matthew 5:48)

Evil agents try to defile you or get you to defile yourself in some way, and there are so many ways. They will even sin **with** you to defile you so their arrow can hit. That could have been their entire plan in the first place—to defile you so they can attack you *spiritually*.

They steal virtue, glory, stars, gifts, blessings and destinies. They can steal so much more spiritually than a simple physical robbery.

Lady saints, not every guy that wants sex from you actually wants sex. The sex is the method by which you will sin and become defiled. After that, you are an easy target for evil arrows. So many people's lives are jacked after having illegal sex. But do they realize it? Do they put these two things together? Like, ever?

It's not like it happens that very moment, or the next day or next week--- all the time. But it can be immediate. Sometimes that sin-guilt you feel also includes the remorse because of the loss of glory or some other spiritual gift or blessing that you need to conduct your life successfully.

One young lady just realized that her entire life changed to the negative three years ago when she went to a fortuneteller. It's not always obvious; sometimes it is very subtle. Three years ago, and she is just realizing it. How about you? What changed? What did you do that was a sin, but you may not have repented, or you didn't even realize it was a sin or it defiled you?

Sex may not be the goal, but means to the end game. Illegal sex may be the defilement that is needed to ruin or steal a person's glory, destiny, or their very life. Evil arrows against you to take down your life, ruin your success, or block your blessings that the Lord has for you.

If it doesn't hit, it is going back to them. It is coming back.

That is one of the reasons you do not sin, try not to sin, and if we do sin, repent quickly when you do. It is why the Holy Spirit alerts you to sin, convicts you of sin, so you can repent quickly and get out of devil territory and devil shooting range for fiery darts, evil arrows and demonic curses.

If hit with evil arrows, then fight back in spiritual warfare; we don't take this to the flesh, You can't say, "Well, Lord, *they started it.* God knows who started it. You are not instigating the curse, you are not the person who is starting the curse, but you are just not letting it land on you or hurt you. **You haven't started the war, but you are defending yourself.**

We don't start wars without god's permission, or His say-so, and first counting up **the cost.** Wars are spiritual; we don't start wars out of our flesh.

What Just Happened?

What just happened?

If your report is something like this: Woke up this morning and things were different, really different. That pain in my *wherever*, doesn't seem to go away. Never felt like this before, physically, emotionally. Feel blah. Blue. What's the use? … then this new state of mind, or state of being could all be from an evil arrow, or multiple evil arrows.

There are signs to recognize the presence of wicked arrows in a life:

1. Sudden physical weakness and sickness. *Woke up like this.*

2. Sudden or very strong urge to sin. When you are suddenly doing things that you would never do, things you hate, suspect evil arrows.

3. Trigger dreams are evil arrows. People have simply died after having certain dreams. Others become lethargic or depressed and can't seem to get it together after an evil arrow. An evil arrow can come in the form of a dream. It can come in the form of an evil summons, or an evil call.

Have you heard your name called, but no one is there? If you know that you are not Samuel and that is not God, then **don't answer it**; it is an evil arrow. Evil instructions follow after that call. **Do not follow the evil instructions whether you actually <u>hear</u> the instructions audibly or not**. State with your powerful mouth that you will not obey any evil instructions, in the Name of Jesus.

4. Sudden lack of interest in the things of God. This may include interest in or being drawn to the dark side.

5. *What is moving in your body?* Do you feel as if something is moving or crawling in your body? That's because of an evil arrow, which may include evil spiritual food eaten in the dream.

6. Feeling hot, and it's not menopause, **and** you're not even a woman.

7. Feeling like your life force has been drained out of you.

8. Reproach, rejection, hatred; people turning against you, or avoiding you for no reason.

9. Sudden change in your children into disobedience and rebellion. That evil arrow may have hit the house and the family or certain susceptible children in the family.

10. Suddenly everything changes in your business. It is an arrow into that business.

11. The *Spirit of error* can be introduced through evil arrows, causing a person to make errors, poor decisions, and costly mistakes and choices.

These are evidences that a wicked arrow has been fired and that that arrow is carrying out its evil assignment.

Pull It Out!

It was either the third grade or the fourth grade, when Johnny Lang sat behind Gary Adkins in class, and I sat behind Johnny. Johnny was a prankster in school, always devising mischief. For some reason, one particular day, after going to the front of the classroom to sharpen his big red pencil that we practiced writing letters and even cursive on the wide-lined, double-lined, newsprint style paper, Johnny came back to his desk. As he walked back to his desk, I saw mischief on his face that day.

Gary also went up to sharpen his pencil. He sat in front of Johnny. We were all going up in order, but the teacher had started from the back of the class. Neither Johnny nor Gary was very studious, but Gary was more serious and was at least trying to learn. Both took this pencil sharpening activity as a chance to move about the room and not be stuck in a chunky wooden desk.

Johnny got back to his seat before Gary because we went in order. I had already sharpened my red pencil and was seated in my desk. I saw Johnny sit back down but in a strange way leaned forward with his right arm out in front of him, with that pencil upright and his hand resting on the seat of Gary's desk chair.

Mrs. Quarles was monitoring the pencil sharpening line, as we had one old-fashioned, wall-mounted rotary pencil sharpener. So, she didn't see what I saw.

But knowing that Johnny is a prankster, I thought he'd show the sharp pencil and then Gary would see it, and push it away and they'd laugh and that would be that.

But no!

Suddenly Gary is screaming, and that big red pencil was stuck in Gary's right buttock. He jumped from his desk and, there was a pencil stuck in his backside. Yes, there really was a pencil stuck in his right rear cheek, and through his trousers and whatever else he was wearing under that, that day.

Gary was immediately taken to the school doctor; yes, we had a doctor then, *and* a school nurse; we had it like that. Someone had to pull that out; it can't just stay there. Aside from the pain and the embarrassment, the poison from the lead in that pencil could get into Gary's bloodstream.

Johnny left the room with Gary and the teacher, but Johnny was marched to the principal's office.

Gary missed the rest of that week from class, and we never saw Johnny again, but oddly, no one missed him. It was rumored that they *moved*, which may be a euphemism for he got expelled from school.

Evil arrows, unlike sharpened red lead pencils are invisible, but they hurt, and they do a lot of damage. Once an evil arrow strikes and enters a person, you don't just leave it there; someone, somehow must pull it out.

How do you get it out?

Back to Sender?

Ideally, it would be better defensively that the arrow never hits or sticks, versus having to remove it. So, if we are praying sorts, we can pray about these arrows prior to feeling any hurt, pain, loss, devastation, affliction, or worse in our lives. So many argue saying that we shouldn't pray **return to sender prayers**, but my Bible shows me where it is indicated.

Yes, God is our defender, but we don't just sit on our haunches and get hit by evil arrows as if we are the target and the witches and warlocks are in target practice. We are also not ducking like Neo in the *Matrix* to let it pass by you, because it could hit or hurt someone else, as in collateral damage.

Saints, this is what intercession is about; we are praying for others so evil arrows don't hit them, especially if arrows intended for us may hurt them. We may not specifically say those words, but in essence that is what we are praying for when we intercede for others because we are our brother's keeper. When we are praying in the Spirit we could be interceding, as well.

You also are not letting it hover in your spiritual environment waiting for the best day and the best way to descend upon you or anyone we are praying for with affliction, death, or whatever evil it was sent to accomplish. Arrows intended for us may hit those in our bloodline and or anyone who is physically close to us, socially close to us, or anyone that we may be in business with. If we don't send back evil arrows, then we can, without realizing it, be an *access point* to others that we know so that evil intended for us can also hit and hurt them.

The work of evil arrows is not always fast; a person could get hit by an arrow this year and may not notice that anything is wrong in their life until next year. It could take days, weeks, months, years – years of sorrow and torture, and confusion wondering *what happened?* Spiritual food eaten in the dream is time bomb food. You could have eaten it --, whenever, but when it is activated, it could cause sudden afflictions. What has changed? What is different?

An evil arrow is what is different.

Whatever the enemy programmed into the arrow, and whatever timing the enemy has programmed into that arrow, without your prayers, or the Mercy of God, that is what will happen. This is why we ought to always pray. Man ought to always repent, and we should also intercede and pray for others.

Because of the time component, some don't know if they've been hit by an arrow (or multiple arrows), or that damage is slowly being done daily to their body and or life, career, business, marriage, spouse, family, or to their children.

Can't Tell

Some just don't know, and won't believe either that witchcraft exists or that evil arrows can be created and can be launched against even unsuspecting folks. (that's another whole story).

As said before, it doesn't matter that you don't believe in witchcraft. The person who is practicing it has to believe in it. You don't practice other world religions, do you? Yet, they still exist.

Folks, it is not just the Galatians, there are people and entire people groups who are bewitched. If you think back over your life, you may realize times that you were blinded to truth, blinded to facts and couldn't even see things that were right in front of your face.

I recall a story that I've told before, but now I am realizing something else about it. The world says that we only see things when we are ready, but, saints of God, sometimes we can't see things because we've been spiritually blinded. If we have been bewitched not to see a thing that should be blatantly obvious, or is obvious to everyone else around us, but we can't see it, you most likely have been bewitched. You are under somebody's spell, and I'm not kidding.

Who did the bewitching? Depends. Depends on who knows how to do that evil thing, or who it will benefit. Might you not be surprised at how many teenagers are witches? Parents, might you wonder what is wrong with your daughter, why she can't see that the guy she's so crazy about is a total jerk? Parents might wonder, why can't he see that the girl he wants to dedicate all his love, life, and time to is not worthy of him?

Because there has been some bewitchment.

If a witch can bewitch in order to bewitch, or to further bewitch they'll do that, too. The Galatians were bewitched to do the bidding of one Simon the Sorcerer.

In my case, I was dating some unworthy fellow and my friends sat me down to dinner with him present to tell me what a this that or the other he was, but I didn't hear anything they were saying. I just enjoyed the meal like an air brain. They never repeated their words to me about this guy ever again, but suddenly a year later, I heard and understood what they were saying. Wow! It took me a year or more to finally **HEAR** what they were saying. Now, I am convinced that I had been bewitched by this fellow and wasted so much time "dating" him--, or whatever it was that we were doing.

I know of another man whose sister is his bewitcher and she has convinced him that witches don't exist, while she is one. This man also believes that, and that witchcraft doesn't exist and if you don't believe in it, it can't affect you. Dude is so wrong.

This man shows EVERY sign of witchcraft attack as his sister dismantles his life because of sibling jealousy--, she wants his money. The story of this man is expounded on in my book, **Blindsided: Has the Old Man Bewitched You?** This fellow's story is not the main story of that book, but it is mentioned in it.

Vengeance Is the Lord's

The wicked will not rule the land of the
godly, for then the godly might be
tempted to do wrong. (Psalm 125: NLT)

He will make your innocence radiate
like the dawn, and the justice of your
cause will shine like the noonday sun.
(Psalm 37:6 NLT)

Whatever the case, your reaction
and response to being bewitched or sent
evil arrows will be based on your soul's
prosperity and how much God and Holy
Spirit you have on board. Will you just
walk away, thankful that you got out of
that situation, or will you go all ballistic
and in full revenge mode?

However, if the person who was to
be cursed prays **back to sender prayers,
it's coming back on the sender.**
Especially if they prayed in faith; it is

going to go back to the sender. It will go back anyway for reasons we will discuss later in this book. But, it will definitely go back sooner, doing far less damage, if you pray that in faith.

Back to sender is legal, it is legitimate, it is Scriptural, and it is our right.

Vengeance is the Lord's.

YES IT IS; I fully agree with that.

But we can ask God for what we want. It is up to God if He will let what we want to happen, happen. The key here is to remain Scriptural, remain Biblical in what we are asking God.

The Word says in John that *If you abide in Me and My Word abides in you, you can ask what you will, and it shall be done; it will be given.* **So, as long** as our request is Scriptural, and we meet the conditions of having what we pray for, God will say, *Yes* to our prayers.

Vengeance is the Lord's. Yes it is: God says He will contend with those who contend with you.

Vengeance is the Lord's. Why, yes, it is, God told them to utterly destroy the enemy (Deuteronomy 20:17).

Vengeance is the Lord's. The Word says that the iniquity of the Amorites was not yet full, implying that when it was full, then God would judge the Amorites.

Vengeance is the Lord's – do you know how many weapons the Lord has in His armory? What do you think those weapons are for? Weapons are not for forgiveness.

Weapons are for WAR. They are for judgment; they are for battles and war; they are for taking the enemy out.

For though we walk in the flesh, we do not war after the flesh. The weapons of our warfare are given by God; they are not carnal.

For though we walk in the flesh, we do not war after the flesh: (For the weapons of our warfare are not carnal, but mighty through God to the pulling down of strong holds; (2 Corinthians 10:3-4)

Saints of God; the weapons of **our** warfare are not carnal; they are not manmade; they are not of the flesh. In order to fight spiritual battles, we need spiritual weapons.

Finally, be strong in the Lord and in his mighty power.

Put on the full armor of God, so that you can take your stand against the devil's schemes.

For our struggle is not against flesh and blood, but against the rulers, against the authorities, against the powers of this dark world and against the spiritual forces of evil in the heavenly realms.

Therefore put on the full armor of God, so that when the day of evil comes, you may be able to stand your ground, and after you have done everything, to stand.

Stand firm then, with the belt of truth buckled around your waist, with the breastplate of righteousness in place,

and with your feet fitted with the readiness that comes from the gospel of peace.

In addition to all this, take up the shield of faith, with which you can extinguish all the flaming arrows of the evil one.

Take the helmet of salvation and the sword of the Spirit, which is the word of God.

And pray in the Spirit on all occasions with all kinds of prayers and requests. With this in mind, be alert and always keep on praying for all the Lord's people. (Ephesians 6:10-18 NIV)

God has many weapons in His armory. God is a consuming fire. God has warrior angels. The Lord is a man of war; the Lord is His name. (Exodus 15:3)

Written

Things are written down for many different reasons. Most folks write things down if they want to make sure you get it right--, things such as grocery lists, or other instructions. Teachers are especially proficient in this. People write things down when they, themselves, don't want to forget. People write things down for posterity's sake. I write many things down because I've had to look all over the place to find out information because it is not in any one place. I write these things down to share with others, so they don't have to look all over creation to find information.

My pastor would call the type of information that I often seek, from the *"book of the elders,"* which is not really a book. It is information that may or may not be commonly known, but it is not written down concisely anywhere. So, **God has given me the charge to write these things down**. This is why you see many books on relevant subjects for the Body of Christ, that they may not lack knowledge in matters of spiritual warfare, and deliverance. It is to edify the Body and glorify God, not me.

People write things down when they get tired of *saying* the same thing over and over. Or if they are weary of watching the same thing happening over and again. It's for our learning, it's for our education; it is for our edification. If the person who needs to learn it is not *getting it*, it is written down for them. This way they can read it.

So, God had the things in the Bible written down for us. I say, let him with an eye to see: **READ,** or let him listen if it is being read or spoken to him.

It is written that a pit digger will fall in his own pit.

Return to sender.

It is written that the rolling stone will roll on the one who is rolling it.

Return to sender.

It is written that the wicked will fall into their own nets, their own traps, their own pits. Well, at least the psalmist prayed that, and knowing that if we abide in the Lord and His Word abides in us, the answers to our prayers are Yes, and Amen.

I know that the LORD will maintain the cause of the afflicted, *and* the right of the poor. (Psalm 140:12)

Keep me from the snares *which* they have laid for me, and the gins of the workers of iniquity.

Let the wicked fall into their own nets, whilst that I withal escape. (Psalm 141:9-10)

When my spirit was overwhelmed within me, then thou knewest my path. In the way wherein I walked have they privily laid a snare for me. (Psalm 142:3)

And of thy mercy cut off mine
enemies, and destroy all them that
afflict my soul: for I *am* thy servant.
(Psalm 143:12)

We shall not be afraid of the arrows that
fly at noonday... (Psalm 91:5-7)

Whatever is written in the Word of
God is how it works, it is how it will be.
Jesus confirmed it over and again even in
His temptations, ***"It is written."***

Whoso diggeth a pit shall fall therein:
and he that rolleth a stone, it will return
upon him. (Proverbs 26:27)

Are you digging a pit for someone?
Maybe God and the Earth don't like the
Earth being dug up for evil. The Earth was
made to glorify God and to serve man; it
wasn't made for evil. Maybe the digging
of an evil pit or untimely, evil grave is
appalling to God, so ***it is written*** in
Scriptures what will happen if that is
done. God will balance that thing out and
fill in the ground again.

- I'm not your candidate, in the
  Name of Jesus. Let that plan

backfire on the digger. Return to sender.

Thinking about rolling a stone? Maybe the stone doesn't want to roll or be moved out of its place. Therefore, that rolling stone is coming back; back to sender, back to the roller.

Vengeance is the Lord's.

War In Heaven

My Bible says that a war broke out in Heaven. A certain one among the Cherubim got kicked out of Heaven and 1/3 of the *stars* came with him. He fell like lightning from Heaven--, to Earth.

So, there is no longer war **in Heaven.** But there is warfare on Earth and in the spiritual realms, because this certain Cherub is war-like and likes to keep some mess going. This Cherub likes to hurt Creation and attempts to hurt the Creator by hurting what He created. This Cherub likes to be rebellious and disobey God. There is warfare on Earth and in spiritual realms, else we wouldn't need spiritual armor and spiritual weapons.

God ended the war in Heaven, but some are slow learners and that's why there are still skirmishes here on Earth and in other spiritual realms because that particular slow-learning Cherub is still fighting God's creation--- *us*.

Yes, he employs evil human agents against us, because *spirits* don't have bodies, and without a body, here, there is no physical authority to do things in the Earth. But we don't take the war against flesh and blood, even though evil human agents are being used, because this is spiritual warfare.

Angry At the Wicked

Are you still arguing about whether to pray return to sender prayers or not? Vengeance is the Lord's. I'm agreeing with Scripture; vengeance is the Lord's.

God is angry at the wicked every day.

God deals with folks, and people, and entities, according to their hearts --- if they have hearts. God deals with them according to the intentions of their hearts, their wishes either for or against His people – you.

They are sending evil arrows? We've got a shield of faith to quench those fiery darts of the evil one. But a shield can also cause a ricochet, then like a boomerang, it's coming back.

Vengeance is the Lord's:

If you   let someone stay in your house and honored them, and treated them very well, like a guest, even. You supported them in every way, gave them a position of honor ---, say--, chief worship leader, made sure they were adorned and beautiful, **but they just turned on you and started a war**, what would you do? The nerve! and in your house; what would you do?

I'm talking about God's House; I'm talking about Heaven and Satan's uprising against God.

God is full of Mercy and He is very forgiving. You're human and you're working on forgiveness, but the goodness that God is giving, Mercy, Loving kindness--, any and all of the **Fruits of the Spirit** that is from God to <u>men</u>--, to men and to the *children* of men.

Oh, that men would praise the Lord for His goodness to men and the children of men. Over and again in the Bible – in Psalms 107, for example, this is what it says… Oh that men would praise the Lord for His goodness to men and the *children* of men.

If someone started a war in your house, you may not be so forgiving or very keen to let them stay in your house. Lucifer started a war in God's House, and that cherub was put out.

What if you kicked the person who started a war in our house out, but they are still being war-like, belligerent, conniving, and rebellious, might you not still have a bone to pick with them, or a few more lessons to teach them, especially if they started picking on or attacking your **children**?

For His goodness to men and the children of men – not to demons, devils, and idols. God doesn't like idols; He doesn't play with idols, and neither should we.

Do you recall when the Ark of the Covenant was in the same place knocking down the image of Dagon – that's a clue as to who has the most power.

And the Philistines took the ark of God, and brought it from Ebenezer unto Ashdod.

When the Philistines took the ark of God, they brought it into the house of Dagon, and set it by Dagon.

And when they of Ashdod arose early on the morrow, behold, Dagon was fallen upon his face to the earth before the ark of the Lord. And they took Dagon, and set him in his place again. (1 Samuel 5:1-3...)

God extends His goodness to men and the children of men. His **goodness** is to those who are <u>HIS</u> and those who are good. Else, God is dealing with people according to their own hearts. If your heart is pure, if it is good, then you will see God and you will see Him working on your behalf.

Vengeance is the Lord's.

God's Glory

When God blesses you, no man can get His glory; He wants you to know and acknowledge those blessings came from the Lord. And you give Him praise and honor.

By the same token, when God fights your battles for you, when He defeats your enemies, when He takes them out, He wants you and the enemies to know, that HE did that, not us.

Do you see how many prideful people are in ministry, for example, bragging that they slayed demons, they did this that and the other? No! **God did that.**

This is why Jesus relayed to His Disciples, Marvel not that the demons are subject to you, but that your name is written in the Book of Life.

Notwithstanding in this rejoice not, that the *spirits* are subject unto you; but rather rejoice, because your names are written in heaven. (Luke 10:20)

Vengeance is the Lord's.

God took those demons out, not a human. Spiritual deliverance is from the Lord, not from a human. Man does not get this glory, because it is God's Glory.

It is blasphemous to attempt to give God's glory to a devil, demon, idol, or false *god*; they didn't save you either. Neither do they have a Heaven to put you in, but they surely have access and a direct path to Hell.

Dumb & Dumber

So, the thing that a person sent to afflict another, kill another, or to hurt a person will come back on them because it is written. It is written that that is the outcome of this particular behavior and sin. The sin of that witchcraft , and the sending of those evil arrows will affect the sender. Once that arrow comes back or the spell backfires, the first thing that generally happens is the person who sent the curse that didn't hit is they are going to go a little bit crazy; they will begin to go mad. They begin to go crazy. How many times have you heard a person say, *Oh, that crazy witch*. Over time, it is bound to happen.

Witchcraft is sin, and unrepented sin can make a person descend into madness.

If someone has the nerve to send a curse or evil arrows against you and it doesn't alight because you are walking upright before the Lord, **IT IS COMING BACK TO THE SENDER**—automatically.

I won't get into how witches create curses or send out evil arrows, but we can figure it out by reading the Bible and by help of the Holy Spirit. The Word of God says:

Thou art snared with the words of thy mouth, thou art taken with the words of thy mouth. (Proverbs 6:2)

If words can snare, trap, and create nets, then we can deduce that evil traps are created by words. Thou art SNARED, entrapped. by the words of your own mouth--- witchcraft words. Curses and spells are words, that is, they are created by words. Curses that didn't alight came

61

back and bit the sender and ensnared the sender.

> Death and Life are in the power of the tongue--- those that love it will eat the fruit thereof. (Proverbs 18:21)

You are just defending yourself when you find yourself under spiritual attack. You are not the evil human agent who started this. You are not the witch who decided to send evil arrows, nor are you the one that was hired to send evil arrows, *right*? And you are not the one who hired someone to do it. But it is a *but they started it* kind of thing. You are not instigating the curse, but you are also not letting it land on you and rest and reside there, waiting for the day that it will take action and hurt your life, or take you out.

You haven't started a war, but you are defending yourself.

Return to sender is part of your defense.

Not Targets, Masterpieces

Yes, God is our defender, but we don't just sit on our haunches and get hit by evil arrows as if we are targets and the witches and warlocks are in target practice.

We are fearfully and wonderfully made. We are God's masterpieces. We are crowned with Glory and Honor. We are called to be priests and kings. We have been gifted with many gifts of the Spirit. We are not old used tin cans for target practice for witches and warlocks, and *what not.* Wise people do not put what is precious into worthless things. We are not worthless things to be attacked or shot at; we are very valuable to God.

We are precious in the eyes and the plan of God. We are the apple of God's eye. He loves us and nothing can take us out of His hand. So, if we are in God's hand and someone is shooting evil arrows at us, then they are shooting arrows at God. God says He will contend with those that are contending with you.

Vengeance is the Lord's.

God calls us Hepzibah and, Beulah land. Hepzibah means, *my delight is in her,* Beulah land means, *married or bride.* He sent His only begotten Son to come here and die for us, so do you think He will just let somebody just keep hurting us?

No.

The Lord God gives us a way out of trouble.

Jesus came to die for us to get us out of captivity and redeem our souls from hell. So don't you think He won't avenge the resident evil bully Cherub on Earth that fell from Heaven. He is still bullying people on Earth and in spiritual realms if he is messing with us? God says that He will rebuke and reprove kings for our sakes. God will take them out. He will arise and He will contend with those who are contending with us.

We are to be the Bride of Christ. If someone was messing with your Bride, or your spouse, you'd have to be a very bad groom to not defend Her.

We are amazing creations; we are not for target practice; whatever is shot at us is coming back.

You wouldn't let someone ding your shiny car, TP your house, or bully your kid. What thing could you create and then allow someone to hurt it or destroy it? Even more when it is a person that you love and have charge over. Even more when it is you who belongs to God and you are under fire, being attacked by evil arrows.

Say It

But we have to open our mouths and SAY what we desire to happen. We have to decree and declare. We have to at least say STOP to the devil, else, it will be as if we are *agree*ing with what he is doing. The Lord will hear our prayers and our cries. The angels of the Lord will respond to the voice of the Word of God.

If little Billy is picking on his *littler* sister, won't she say, "STOP Billy"? Man, she's three. We are not three years old; we can open our mouths, can't we? We can pray and do warfare, can't we?

Ouch is not a proper response in warfare. Warfare is a proper response in warfare.

What David Asked For

You just couldn't ask God to do anything terrible to anybody, could you? Not even somebody who is doing something terrible to you? What if they are doing something terrible to your children? Let's see, what did David ask God to do to his enemies, in Psalm 109?

Do not keep silent,
O God of my praise!
For the mouth of the wicked and the
mouth of the deceitful
Have opened against me;
They have spoken against me with a
lying tongue.
They have also surrounded me with
words of hatred,
And fought against me without a cause.

David is talking about human enemies – but we are asking the Lord for defense against spiritual enemies. The spiritual enemies are the powers behind the evil human agents. If we shut down their power, then the battle is won. David talks about the mouth of the wicked: this is witchcraft, evil human agents who are enchanting, incanting, casting spells against God's people, **with their mouths.**

And they hide to shoot at the upright in heart. Who are those people? Occultic and witchcraft people hide.

God is our defense. So, do you think He's going to let people just shoot at you, without doing anything? Of course, not; that would not be defending us.

What will He do? God can't do a lot of things in the Earth--, even a lot of things we want Him to do until we agree with Him. We open our mouths and agree with God, so He has permission to move on our behalf.

First thing, know that evil arrows can go back. It is going back in order for these people to learn to stop doing evil by having what they are doing to others to happen to them. God wants to redeem people. Maybe if the intended affliction happens to them, they will learn and stop that evil behavior.

God is angry with the wicked every day.

If this arrow coming back on them causes them to stop--, if this works that tells God, that they still have consciences; they are still human and not reprobate. Maybe that heart of stone that they have right now can be turned into a heart of flesh. Repentance can happen. A soul is won. Glory to God.

If they don't repent, if they don't change their ways, then we know that we are dealing with a *pharaonic spirit, a seared conscience, or a reprobate mind. If this is who they are and are not willing to repent and change, then God will deal with them as they are. To the pure all things are pure, to the defiled, all things are defiled.* The pharaonic spirit is hard-hearted; whatever they are sending out, they won't stop. Death is the only thing that stops them. God will deal with them; He deals with people according to their own hearts.

To the faithful you show yourself
faithful; to those with integrity you show
integrity. To the pure you show yourself
pure, but to the crooked you show
yourself shrewd.

You rescue the humble,
but you humiliate the proud. (Psalm
18:25-27)

Gotta Deal With It

Do you plan to deal with wickedness, an evil *spirit*, or power differently than how God says to deal with them? God is dealing with them as wicked entities, but you want to be all nice and forgiving and let them continue to run all over you, oppress you, destroy your business and oppress your family? You want to take them a lemonade?

Are you planning to deal with them differently than how the Word says to deal with them? The Word tells us what to do. When God says go do this and so, you go do that.

We don't know how to pray as we ought. Sometimes we don't know how to pray or what to pray, but when God says pray a certain way, you do that. When God says don't pray for that evil person, then you stop. When the Spirit of God takes over, praying through us in utterances that you don't even understand, then you let Him.

Do you think God is going to let some evil, demonic spirit or power just whip up on you? what kind of God would He be? What kind of king doesn't defend His kingdom? What kind of Father doesn't protect His children? God is not spiritually deadbeat.

It's coming back. That evil arrow is coming back on the sender. You might as well agree with God sooner, rather than waiting until later. Return to sender.

As you're taking care of your family and your house, will you just let anything in? Of course not. And whatever may get in, you defend your house against that. You see an *ant*? It's got to go. A roach or other insect or varmint? It's got to go. Return to sender.

A *Divinator?*

If you think about it -- God versus a divinator? Who do you think is sending evil arrows? Witches, warlocks, sorcerers and the like. Do you think God is going to sit back and watch that and do nothing? God versus a divinator? No contest, really, unless you've decided to agree with the divinator by being in sin, continuing in sin, not repenting, saying nothing, or doing nothing.

Nope, it's going back. Else, whatever is sent against you will succeed. Sooner, rather than later, we need evil arrows sent against us to go back.

Don't make God have to judge both of you by agreeing with a divinator.

However, as God is teaching your hands to war and your fingers to fight, you must do something, not nothing. After all, that's what the whole armor is for.

Those who shoot privily at the upright in heart are enemies of God, and yours as well. You are the upright, *right*? Then the curse can't even hit you.

If you are **not** the upright, then repent and get RIGHT with God.

But if you are doing nothing, and plan to do nothing because you couldn't possibly pray that prayer because those people are your friends, or your family--, you know them. We are praying against the powers they employ; we are not praying against flesh and blood.

God is long suffering. As long as you want to suffer, He may let you if you want to do nothing, waiting for God to fix it, saying, *God's got this.* Yeah, God's got it, but He is waiting for you to **state your case**; state what you want to happen regarding what has got you or trying to get you. Yes, there is a "case" in the spirit that has been opened against you, else the enemy would not be able to be doing any thing at all to you. (Read **Evil Petition** by this author.)

God avenges all disobedience in your obedience. If you are not walking upright before the Lord or if you are not sincerely repentant for your sins, then He's not getting in that. He can't avenge you if you are disobedient because He'd have to judge you along with your enemies. The fact that He doesn't is Mercy. He is giving you time and space to repent.

Confusion

The return of the evil arrow is built into the sin of witchcraft and the sending of the arrow in the first place.

When evil starts fighting evil, that is confusion. Confusion in the enemy's camp is as good as anyone would want it.

- Let my enemies fight each other.
- Lord, raise up and adversary against my enemies, in the Name of Jesus.

Saints of God, the adversary that the Lord raises up as God teaches you spiritual warfare could be you. Didn't David have to go out against Goliath? God is teaching your hands to war, and your fingers to fight.

Then David Said

In return for my love they are my accusers, But I *give myself to* prayer. Thus they have rewarded me evil for good, And hatred for my love. (Psalm 109:4-5)

Yes, these arrow-shooting evil human agents could be people you know. We don't war against flesh and blood, but we see the behaviors they exhibit and discern what *spirits* to attribute their behaviors to so we know how to pray accordingly.

David continues in Psalm 109:

Set a wicked man over him,
And let an accuser stand at his right hand.
When he is judged, let him be found guilty, And let his prayer become sin. Let his days be few,
And let another take his office.

Let his children be fatherless,
And his wife a widow. (Psalm 109:6-9)

This is Biblical. This is David, a man after God's own heart. No one is asking you to pray a prayer this harsh, but no one is stopping you either. David did it. *God loved Him some David.*

Let his children continually be
vagabonds, and beg;
Let them seek *their bread* also from their
desolate places.
Let the creditor seize all that he has,
And let strangers plunder his labor.
Let there be none to extend mercy to
him,
Nor let there be any to favor his
fatherless children.
Let his posterity be cut off,
And in the generation following let their
name be blotted out.

Let the iniquity of his fathers be
remembered before the Lord,
And let not the sin of his mother be
blotted out.
Let them be continually before the Lord,
That He may cut off the memory of them
from the earth;

Because he did not remember to show
mercy, (Psalm 109:6-16)

Not showing Mercy is a hallmark
of demonic and satanic curses and spells.
There is no Mercy in them; there is no
Mercy in the dark kingdom.

But persecuted the poor and needy man,
That he might even slay the broken in
heart.
As he loved cursing, so let it come to
him;
As he did not delight in blessing, so let it
be far from him. (Psalm 109: 17-18)

As said before, God deals with
people according to their own hearts.

As he clothed himself with cursing as
with his garment,
So let it enter his body like water,
And like oil into his bones.
Let it be to him like the garment which
covers him,
And for a belt with which he girds
himself continually.
Let this *be* the Lord's reward to my
accusers,

And to those who speak evil against my
person. (Psalm 109:18-20)

You see above, *they* are still
speaking. This is not about gossip,
rumors, and hearsay. This is not about
curse words and profanity; this is about
evil enchantments and creating curses
with intention and evil words. This is
about casting spells and sending evil
arrows to people. A speaking voice can be
powerful, even inspirational, but when a
speaker is evil and repeats lies and lies and
propaganda over and over that speaker is
CASTING SPELLS, even if he is doing it
in public, at a microphone, to a crowd.
**The boldest witches do it in front of
people.**

These people mean no good. The
public ones are dictators, would-be
dictators, manipulators, criminals, and
authoritarian leaders. There is no need to
lie if you are for good. The liars are from
the pit of hell.

Which imagine mischiefs in their
heart; continually are they gathered

together for war. They have
sharpened their tongues like a
serpent; adders' poison is under their
lips. Selah. (Psalm 140:1-3)

Folks, these people are not wiser
than God; they are not ahead of God. All
of this has already been seen and dealt
with in the Bible. David saw it and it was
written down so we could learn from it
and not be victims also. If you need
discernment, pray to receive the Holy
Spirit. If you have the Holy Spirit, pray for
more discernment.

Let not an evil speaker be established in
the earth: evil shall hunt the
violent man to overthrow *him*. (Psalm
140:11)

Help me, O Lord my God!
Oh, save me according to Your mercy,
That they may know that this *is* Your
hand—
That You, Lord, have done it! (Psalm
109:26-27)

Again, God wants you to know
that **HE** did this. David is acknowledging
that God protected him, God delivered

him. We are not doing this alone. We have the authority, but we don't have the **power** within us like God has. God is all-knowing and He has all power; Power belongs to God.

Let them curse, but You bless;
When they arise, let them be ashamed,
But let Your servant rejoice.
Let my accusers be clothed with shame,
And let them cover themselves with
their own disgrace as with a mantle.
I will greatly praise the Lord with my
mouth;
Yes, I will praise Him among the
multitude.
For He shall stand at the right hand of
the poor,
To save *him* from those who condemn
him. (Psalm 109:18-31)

David prayed this; he prayed strong prayers. David, a man after God's own heart prayed like this – it's Scriptural and it is in the Bible.

Forgive Them

But we are supposed to forgive, you may say.

Yes, we forgive humans. Forgiveness is for humans; we forgive people. We forgive them, yes forgive folks, if not for them, do it for yourself. But look closely at that passage and see what we are supposed to forgive people for. We forgive the taking of tangible, physical items. I see nowhere in the passages that we are supposed to forgive people for stealing other more important and weightier things, such as life, destiny, marriage, family, children, education, reputation, *inheritance.* I believe Jesus didn't want us tied to physical property to the degree that we would not forgive people for taking it. In the Old Testament you weren't even supposed to sell land you inherited, for example. Therefore you should not let it be taken from you.

Forgiveness is not for demons, powers, and spiritual wickedness, those entities will NOT be forgiven. If God isn't forgiving them, why would you? You're just going to let everything they are doing against you just slide? How can you?

Demons, devils, idols, spiritual wickedness, rulers, evil principalities, and powers will not be forgiven. Their time is short, and they will be ultimately dismissed into the Lake of Fire that burns with sulfur and brimstone. If God is not forgiving them, then God hasn't forgiven them; then God won't forgive them. They have no way of repenting.

What?

How can they come to God by Jesus Christ? Redemption through Jesus is for mankind, only, not demons and devils and fallen angels.

Furthermore, do you think God will let all those powers do millennia and generations of stealing, killing, and destroying to mankind and His Creation and then just forgive them? If God were going to forgive, He would have already done it and there would be a record somewhere that this has been done, or is possible for them. There isn't, and it is not possible. God forgives when there is repentance. If anyone has not *changed*, or by His Grace, in the process of *changing*, then forgiveness is not possible.

The devil is still evil; his demons are all the same, set in their demonic ways. If they had repented and were no longer demonic, Christians and people in general would have no opposition in our lives. They are not changing, they are not repenting, and there is no forgiveness for demons.

Jesus said, *No **man** comes to the Father, except by Me.*

Demons and devils can't just come into your life unless you've invited them by your words or deeds, unless there is a dimensional access point left carelessly open by an ancestor--, an open spiritual door. They can't just come into your life and do *whatever* in your *house*. If they do and you are aware of their presence, you must put them out of your house and out of your life because the longer they are there, the more they become aggressive and warlike. Be sin free. Repent. And seek deliverance when necessary.

The devil is still looking for people to devour.

Remember, we are not warring against flesh & blood, unless that flesh and blood has chosen to be joined, irreversibly in covenant with demonic powers and is unrepentant. In that case they risk going down with the evil ship that they've boarded.

Ultimately, that is between them and God whether they will embrace evil to the point of never repenting, so they themselves *become* evil, also. But saints have the authority to conduct spiritual warfare. Actually, as stated, it is expected of us.

Send Them Back

Evil arrows are flying, and they are usually person-specific unless it's for a group or a population that you happen to be a part of. An arrow can hit a house. An arrow can hit a business. An arrow can hit the building that a business is in.

The devil is the one who influences the evil imagination of man and drives them to send out an arrow a certain way, or they are told by the demon that they interface with what kind of attack, how, and also *when*.

Arrows are formed specifically to do the damage that the sender wants, but vengeance must come, and vengeance is the Lord's. Those arrows can go back, because *it is written*. Those arrows can go back because you say so. Those arrows can go now, especially if you say so and you have faith for **now**. Especially if you pray, Return to Sender.

- Lord, send every evil arrow back, in the Name of Jesus.
- Roll that stone back, in the Name of Jesus.
- Lord, fill that pit with the digger, in the Name of Jesus.
- Lord, let that net catch the one that spread it, and not me or mine, in the Name of Jesus.

Don't just sit around pretending that there is no arrow, letting it hover in your spiritual environment waiting for the best day and the best way to descend upon you with affliction or your business career, family, spouse, marriage, children, your health or whatever it was sent to destroy.

However, if the person who was to be cursed prays back to sender prayers, it's coming back on the sender. Especially if they pray in faith.

The point of this is that if you plan to formulate a curse or a charm or evil arrow yourself --, **don't do it**.

If you decide to initiate any form of witchcraft against a person, by now you have to know that God hates that. God didn't tell you to do that because that is not how He operates. Witchcraft employs demons from the second heaven to create these arrows, charms and every other kind of evil spiritual weapon. God doesn't make deals with or have His people to make deals with the second heaven. The second heaven is demonic, it is where the seat of Satan is.

God is way above their level, in the Third Heaven and He is not in league with them. So why would you be? God will not send you there to get things and stuff and make deals and covenants with the devil. That is man either sending himself, or getting tricked or trapped into those kinds of deals.

That is where witches and occultists go for power. That is where they go to make weapons against mankind.

God will judge that, and witches are not entering into the Kingdom of Heaven. You know that, *right*?

Moreover, if you want to devise an evil arrow to propel in the direction of a perceived enemy yourself, first consider your state of mind, and your emotions. If you are emotionally charged, that means you are in your flesh. In your flesh dwells no good thing. In your flesh you will co-op with second heaven demons to create the revenge weapon that you may be thinking of, whether you realize you are doing it or not. **<u>Don't do it,</u>** because GOD did not authorize that weapon. That weapon is not sanctioned by God, and mostly because vengeance is the Lord's.

You also don't do it because all your intended victim has to do is be in Christ, and pray against your attacks, whether they use the words, *back to sender* or not, but especially if they do.

Even though you may think this person is a heathen, they may not be; God knows. Don't underestimate another person's spiritual walk out of ignorance, hatred, or in anger.

You may be in unforgiveness, and you haven't forgiven them, and you don't ever plan to forgive them; you think they deserve what you are planning against them. You may think that they are the #1 heathen of all heathens, and that God must certainly be agreeing with you about punishing this person. For that reason, you believe –, no, you think you **know** that the arrow will not only hit, but it will accomplish what you want it to accomplish against the bum who did this, that or the other to you.

And, for some reason you think that God has okayed for you to exact the vengeance, when vengeance is His, not yours, and not ours. Witches think like that.

Yup, witches --, not the people of God. While forming this devil-weapon, you are speaking. If not creating the entire weapon, you are speaking your intent to whomever you've hired, or blindly wished that some hurt or harm would come to so and so as you call them a *so and so.*

Now, you've become an evil speaker. Even if you did it in private. Folks, second-heaven rituals are examples of evil speaking, also.

Let not an evil speaker be established in the earth: evil shall hunt the violent man to overthrow *him.* (Psalm 140:11)

Renounce and denounce that sin and that behavior. Repent & ask God to remove the iniquity. Do it quickly, or it's coming back.

Folks, that arrow will be coming back at YOU, some time, some way, and some day. It's coming back.

You cannot surely think that the evil will shoot at the upright in heart, God's people, and get away with it? The evil speakers will not be established in the Earth.

As my mom used to say, *They may get by, but they won't get away.*

No Weapon

No weapon formed against you shall prosper, And every tongue which rises against you in judgment You shall condemn. (Isaiah 54:1 NKJV)

Every tongue that rises up against you, you can condemn. Witches, enchanters spell-, hex-, and vex-creators who create evil arrows to attack the upright in heart, you can condemn all their work and words. Yes, evil speakers are using **words**.

Saints of God, I don't know how anyone who reads the Bible can't see witches and witchcraft all through it.

- Lord, in the Name of Jesus, I condemn every evil imagination and every enchanting tongue that has risen up against me by the power in the Blood of Jesus. No weapon formed against me shall prosper; I condemn, I condemn, I condemn the words of the evil man against me, in the Name of Jesus.

No weapon formed: SO, we need to be sure that **we** are not *forming* weapons, because vengeance is the Lord's. So, if there are weapons and they turn on us because we are not able to handle them, because we are not supposed to be forming them, then what are we doing? Self-sabotage? Spiritual suicide?

No humans are supposed to be forming weapons—, not even witches and occultists because they are coming back to attack them because **it is written** that it shall not afflict the upright. This is what makes witches and their ilk spiritual outlaws.

Evil arrows are coming back if we send them back. The weapons that the dark kingdom forms will come back on them; they **backfire**.

Weapons can reverse and hurt the owner of that weapon. The bullets/arrows that the weapon sends out can also reverse and come back on the sender.

Witches *form* weapons.

Conversely, we use the weapons that God already has in His armory.

So, we must stop *forming* weapons because we are not witches. That's another reason why vengeance is the Lord's: He does not want you forming weapons, willy nilly, with your dangerous self. The weapons that we have access to should only be used by God, by His warring angels, and by authority and permission of God.

Oops?

Let's say you create some devil weapon in your flesh, using your own imagination in your own hate, in your own envy, in your own jealousy, your own hurt, and your own pain. You've created an evil weapon with your evil words, with your dangerous self.

First you created it in your evil thoughts, then your evil words--, this is why we are to cast down imaginations, so they don't become evil words that become evil weapons. All that person that you are sending it against has to do is say, *Return to sender* and it is definitely coming back at you.

Let's say you launch this weapon. Well, folks, this creates a whole new problem. Firstly, you don't mess with

God's people. Secondly, if you are God's people you don't mess with flesh and blood anyway. And, as importantly, one back to sender will bring it back on your own head.

His mischief shall return upon his own head, and his violent dealing shall come down upon his own pate. (Psalms 7:16)

The new problem is: What is the prayer for the weapon that you created against *yourself*? What can you pray to not be hurt by the weapon you created for another that is now attacking you? Is it, *Nevermind*? Is it *Oops*? Is it *My bad?* No, none of those are prayers.

So, don't do it, because there appears to be no coming back from that.

Is there a *back to intended victim prayer*? Never heard of that, and how many times will an arrow make the circuit, make U-turns, ricochet, or boomerang like a cartoon? It goes east, it turns around and goes back to the west, then does it still stay suspended and come back east when you are ready for it again?

Not hardly.

Does it just sit there until the original victim is not paying attention anymore for a gotcha moment of evil? Back to the west? How many times does it volley or make this circuit?

You may say it depends on how much power is behind it. It depends what kind of altar is propelling it. Yes, to a degree, it does. It depends on what sacrifice is on that altar? Yes, to a degree, it does.

Pray:

- Altar, altar, fight for me. Altar of the Only Living God, I claim the sacrifice of Christ and defeat every other altar working against me, in the Name of Jesus.

Now, saints of God, vengeance is the Lord's because if you are fighting with a brother in the Faith, can you both claim the sacrifice of Christ, and the Blood of Jesus? Of course, not. Christ will not fight against Himself, and God is not the author of confusion. This is why we don't *form* weapons without God's permission. We don't do it because we don't know what we are doing.

This is why we don't start wars without authorization, instruction, and the plan of God. The Fruit of the Spirit is Peace, not war. We are supposed to be for peace not war. There must be balance; we fight when we should, and we fight whom the Lord tells us to fight. We fight in the Spirit. We don't just sit around waiting for God to do it. We fight and we win so that we live to fight another day.

Some of the same folks who would never do spiritual warfare may be in hate and spats with their pew neighbor.

Oh really?

Yes.

There may be two men vying for the same church title, or there is one promotion at work, and they both want it. They are not even civil to one another anymore. Two so-called ladies may be fighting for the same man. They hate each other because of competition. So don't say you don't know how to fight, how to battle, how to war. Don't say you don't do it because everyone does it, especially a soul that is not prospered and well-ordered.

Vengeance is the Lord's.

Unsanctioned warfare is evil. If God did not sanction it; it is demonic and evil.

There Is a Captain

There are spiritual warriors. There are biblical accounts of the same. You may find yourself in that ilk. However, we see all through Scripture that Jesus is the Captain of the Host of the Lord. We know that host to be warrior angels. We also know that there was a war that broke out in Heaven and that there is still war in spiritual realms that requires warrior angels, who have access to and use spiritual weapons.

But there is a Captain. The warrior angels obey the voice of the Word of God. We, too follow the lead of the Captain; Angels don't do their own thing, neither do we do our own thing.

We also don't war against those that we shouldn't war against.

You can look at witches, warlocks, and wizards as those who have <u>defected</u> from the Army of the Lord (if they were ever in it), and are doing their own thing, so they think. But in reality, they are being led by another "captain" who is leading and instructing them on how to make *other* weapons, different weapons and teaching them how to inflict those weapons on humans to afflict them, to steal, kill, and destroy. He's taught them how to make a whole lot of evil weapons, and a sign of a witch is to make them and the willingness to use them, unsanctioned by God, and without Mercy.

Devil weapons don't work on God. If you are in Christ and abiding in Him, you are protected. If you are in the shadow of the Almighty, you are protected. If you are in the Cleft of the Rock, also protected. If you are in the whole armor, protected. Against the Grace of God, there is no law. The devil is a legalist and what he wants to do against any person must be by judgment because that man broke a spiritual law. If you behave as Christ did, there is no law that can capture, torment, hurt, harm, steal from, or kill you.

None of us are perfect, but in Christ, by the Blood of Jesus, we are seen through the eyes of Mercy and Grace by the Lord.

Following the evil one, we may choose to or be enticed into making a devil device or weapon. Devil weapons are a joke to God, but they are no joke to flesh and blood. God will have them in derision (Psalm 2:4).

Devil weapons can be devastating to mankind, if unopposed. Witchcraft is powerful if unopposed; we must oppose it. That is, we must defend ourselves.

Witchcraft weapons, such as evil arrows are dangerous to men, to flesh and blood, yet they are like toys in the Hand of an Almighty God who can crush them at will. Those of us who are *in Christ*, if we are bold and courageous, we can also crush devil weapons. We can disrespect them. We can send them back. We can destroy them with Holy Ghost Fire, or the Thunder Hammer of God. We can shred them with the Razor of the Lord. There are many weapons we have at our disposal to be rid of evil arrows.

But if we do nothing, we could get hit. If we send them love and light back – that's nice, and many think this is the Christian thing to do.

Seriously, would you do that if natural bullets were flying? No, you would duck, seek cover, and if possible, <u>fire back</u>. That is exactly what you would do. Fire back. But if you had no bullets, no weapons of your own, what would you do? You would pick up that rock that was just thrown at you and throw it back at whomever threw it at you. It is a natural reflex. If not, the choice is to just stand there and get stoned to death, shot to death, or killed by enemy arrows.

Lord, forbid.

We don't make weapons because the weapons that humans make are against flesh and blood, and we are flesh and blood. It's only a matter of time before human-made weapons could hurt even the ones who made it. Weapons don't have minds, if they are engineered against flesh and blood, they seek flesh and blood.

Whose?

The weapons don't know, they don't have minds, they can't discern, and they have no loyalty.

If a gun, for example, backfires, then it's lights out for the shooter. The gun doesn't know, *Oh, this is my owner, I'd better not hurt them*. If a weapon is wrestled away from its owner and then aimed at the owner, the gun will fire if that trigger is pulled. The same applies for words; a man can have whatever he says. You say something that is ridiculous, stupid or even self-destructive, your angels can't even change it--, you can have it. If it is not repented of in a timely manner, and especially if it is repeated over and again, you not only can have it, but you **will** also have it.

The *words* that go into evil arrows, are just that—, words. All the same laws apply to words as well because they are weapons. If not sanctioned by God, those words are renegade, and they create destructive devices against flesh and blood.

Praying ***return to sender*** is the same as wrestling a loaded gun out of the hand of a would-be assassin and turning it on the sender while you still have the ability to fire on the enemy that has already fired on you, whether you've been struck or not.

But, we wrestle not against flesh and blood, so stay out of the flesh. That's a major difference in demonic weapons; they surely target flesh and blood.

Automatic?

So, the thing that a person sent to afflict another, kill another, hurt a person will come back on them if they just pray, *return to sender*. And it is coming back for some other reasons, also. Once the spell backfires, the sender may go mad, or crazy. Witchcraft is sin, even *blind witchcraft*.

Why madness?

Being lied to over and again can break a man's spirit. A man's spirit governs his mind. The kind of deception and confusion the devil must instill in a person to deceive them to defect from LIFE and the Source of their own life has to make them mad, eventually. *When they realize how badly they've been deceived, they may descend instantly into madness.*

Not only that, madness is built-in to some evil covenants, so if the evil agent does not effect their goal, yes it's coming back on them and with demonic vengeance. Many times, that evil revenge is madness or starts with madness.

Unrepented sin carries iniquity. What the devil deems as fair game for failed assignments is part of that iniquity, as well as the judgment of God for having committed the sin in the first place.

Yes, arise in your whole spiritual armor and war against spiritual wickedness in high places. Yes, we pray, declare and decree, *back to sender*. But we know, it is up to God if, when, and how He will take down your enemies.

We need to stay prayed up, saints of God:

And know that whatever you do, good or bad, it's coming back to you and it's going back to sender. If we are the sender, guess where it's coming? If we abide in Christ and He abides in us, we can have what we ask. We are just agreeing with the Word, agreeing with God and asking for a speedy outcome to whatever afflictions that have beset us…the pain, the obstacles, the inconveniences, the suffering, the hurt or frustrations that we are going through. It's automatic, it's built in.

With the same measure you give it out, it will be given back to you is a Biblical law.

GOD KEEPS CAREFUL RECORDS.

GOD HATES a false balance and unjust SCALES.

GOD IS A GOD OF BALANCE AND JUSTICE.

GOD IS JUST, else why would we have to give an account when it is all said and done. Because God has records.

The devil has records too, so he can accuse us and get judgments, to do foul things to mankind. (Read my book, **Evil Petition**).

In the comfort of knowing that when your enemies rise up against you,

God will raise up a standard against them, God will fight your battles, God is your banner, He is your defense, He is your refuge, He is a strong tower that the righteous can run into and be safe.

We are not sitting ducks for target practice. As you learn and discern, you don't keep walking in the way of sinners, and mockers, and evil people and do what they say do. You don't even go to where these people hang out unless God *sent* you, and that with protection and grace and anointing. When God sends you, you won't take on their nature or their lifestyle.

But we ourselves don't delve into that evil but we have the opportunity and the right to defend ourselves if it is coming against us.

If you, in a fit of evil, start something that you shouldn't, know that it is coming back. Whatever you dish up— if you start it, and your target says Return to Sender, it's coming back.

By the justness of God, and by the balance in the Kingdom of God, good or bad what you dish up is COMING BACK one way or the other, some day or the other.

Human-made weapons take death out of the hands of God. When man plays God, that is idolatry, when idolatry invites Death, Death becomes the teacher of how to make weapons of destruction and mass destruction.

Jesus said, **I am the Way, the Truth, and the <u>Life</u>**. God appoints the days of a man; all of them are in His hand.

God is about life. God is about Life Eternal.

The devil is about death.

Eyes to See

If you don't see it – you may not realize that you even made a weapon, especially if you are blinded by *rage*.

If you don't have eyes to see, you may not realize that something you created backfired.

Why?

Well, by the Mercy of God, and or the prayers of other saints, it could take a long time to come back or manifest. depending on how long it takes to come back --- if your children are not fully in Christ, it could come back on your children, It could come back on your grandchildren.

You may not be able to see it because you've been bewitched not to see it. You could be looking right at it and not see it. It's like the kid who can't find the orange juice that is right in front of them in the fridge. I mean, it's right there. You've met kids like that, right? You may have one of those. Don't yell at them, teach them, pray for them. Deliverance may be needed, if they can't see, physically see what is right in front of them. All the more critical when they can't see that a reality or a life lesson is right in front of them. Some say that they can't think abstractly – maybe not, but this is a spiritual problem and prayer is indicated. Strong prayer.

Bobby, Jimmy is not your friend.

Why do you say that mom, dad?

Can't you see it, Bobby? He borrows your bike all the time, but you can't use anything of his. He is a taker and a user.

I don't see it, mom, dad.

And Bobby really can't see it.

Some things Bobby can see, or he can see in others, but not in his so-called friend, Jimmy. Jesus said to the people of Jerusalem, you can tell when the sky is lowering, but you missed your visitation. Granted, He was talking about being able to see *physical* things, but not spiritual things. But little Bobby if he can't even see physical things, don't you think spiritual things will escape him?

Being blinded to physical things is a bewitchment, it is a caging of the mind. Better pray.

Bobby can't find his socks that are right there in the sock drawer where they always are. Mom, dad – either of you may say, *Bobby, the socks are right here where we told you they were. If it had been a snake…*

Bobby's parents, I must tell you that it **is** a snake. It is a poisonous venomous, bewitching snake. Do you want to wait until Bobby grows up to find out what he cannot *see*?

We are spirits; should we not be able to see spiritual things, or train ourselves to see spiritual things? Stand back far enough to get whole pictures, big pictures. Yeah, change perspective, back up off of Jimmy who has your ear or pulling your leg or whatever kind of witchcraft he's doing on Bobby. Back up and see him as he is and what he's spitting out. Chances are very good that he is just using words, or it started as just words.

Parents, don't you recall telling your son, *You don't believe everything everybody tells you. Bobby, don't believe everything Jimmy says.* That could have been the beginning of it all.

It may not be Jimmy at all. It could be in your foundation and Bobby is the target of this selective *blindness*, although he has 20/20 vision.

So, an arrow has been sent and it has hit. A bewitching arrow in the case of Bobby. An arrow of affliction in the case of Job. Arrows of death in the case of

anyone who died mysteriously, either
suddenly, or painfully slow.

Do your spiritual work:

- Nullify evil arrows, pull them out,
  and heal the part or parts that it hit.
- Ask the Lord for spiritual surgery
  to immediately remove any arrow
  that has struck you or the person
  you are praying for.
- **Ask the Lord to reverse** the
  effects of these arrows and heal
  you.
- Pray that the Lord will break up the
  evil altar that is sending out these
  evil arrows.

Joshua got God to stop the sun from
setting until he finished the battle and won
it. Can we not also do that in the personal
battles we become embroiled in with the
enemy who is sending evil arrows?
Shouldn't we be so intent on getting evil
arrows out that we say,

- Lord, hold up, hold up – help me get this arrow out, now, in the Name of Jesus.

The Kingdom of Heaven suffers violence and the violent takes it by force. By force, send back every evil arrow. If you want to add the caveat,

- Lord and let it hit them, let it hit my unrepentant enemies; deal with them the way they are dealing with me, in the Name of Jesus.

The Lord knows who is unrepentant and will never stop shooting at you and He knows who will receive Christ and become a brother or sister in the faith.

Invite the Holy Spirit

The prayers I pray are for Protestant Christians; anyone else who prays them without being born again and in Christ may run the risk of making their situation worse.

Lord Jesus, come into my life. I accept You as my Lord and Personal Savior. I believe in my heart You died and rose from the dead to save me. Thank You Lord for saving me, in Jesus' Name.

Lord, fill me with Your Holy Spirit, with evidence of speaking in tongues, in the Name of Jesus.

Amen.

Prayer Points

1. Lord, I repent for my sins and the sins of my ancestors, in the Name of Jesus. Remove all iniquity from my bloodline, in Jesus' Name.

2. I pray for the Mercy of God as I declare judgment on evil arrows and the powers behind those sent against me and what is mine, in Jesus' Name.

3. I fire back every arrow of witchcraft now, in the Name of Jesus.

4. Arrows of reproach, hatred, embarrassment, humiliation, and limitation, backfire, in the Name of Jesus.

5. Tongues--, evil tongues that have risen up to defeat me, catch Fire, in the Name of Jesus.

6. Powers assigned to multiply my problems, you are liars, die, in the Name of Jesus.

7. Every gathering of my mockers, scatter, in the Name of Jesus.

8. Coffin of darkness, on assignment against me, bury your senders, in the Name of Jesus.

9. Arrows fired against my staff of bread, backfire, in the Name of Jesus.

10. Any satanic anointing speaking against me, I break your source of power by the Power in the Blood of Jesus.

11. Powers circulating my name for evil, become powerless and die, in the Name of Jesus.

12. Arrows of envious enemies, backfire, in the Name of Jesus!

13. Arrows from evil manipulators, return to sender, in the Name of Jesus.

14. Covenants behind the battles fighting me, break by the Blood of Jesus.

15. Altars behind evil covenants fighting against me, I crush you with the Thunder Hammer of God.

16. Arrows of pestilence, arrows of pandemic, I am not your candidate, die, in the Name of Jesus.

17. Arrows fired into my house, my home, my business or the building in which I do business, return to sender, in the Name of Jesus.

18. Arrows fired against my family, abort mission against us, and return to sender, in the Name of Jesus.

19. Lord, in the Name of Jesus, I seal this word, these prayers, decrees, declarations and deliverance across every realm, era, age, timeline, past present and future, to infinity. I seal it with the Blood of Jesus and the Holy Spirit of God.

20. Let every backlash intended against these words, these prayers, the author, anyone reading this book, praying these prayers, making these decrees, declarations and receiving deliverance, let it go back to sender, without Mercy and to infinity, in the Name of Jesus.

21. Lord, stop any attempts of reorganization or regrouping of evil networks against the people of God involved in these prayers and deliverance, in the Name of Jesus.

What Have You Done?

This book is to especially warn you to **repent** because of what you *may have* already sent out, unaware that you did it. If you purposefully or inadvertently sent out an evil arrow that may not have hit and it was returned to you, you may be why you suffering. It is possible that your suffering may be because of some weapon <u>you</u> formed, created, or *wished* on someone, but it didn't hit, so it came back to you.

Saints, this is why we forgive 70 X 7, and this is why we repent. This is why we walk in the Spirit so we don't fulfill the lust of the flesh. **Revenge is a lust of the flesh.**

Like what? How did I create an evil weapon? By any evil words, even *blind witchcraft* words, you may have uttered in unforgiveness, hate, jealousy, animosity, competition, bitterness, greed, envy --- this is why we stay out of the flesh. This is why we shut our own mouths, so we don't create weapons against others--, because we are not witches. When carnal weapons against flesh and blood are created that God didn't authorize, we sin. We don't do that. We are not witches. And also, because whatever we send out is coming back.

Repent of creating weapons. Evil weapons. Unauthorized weapons. Flesh weapons. Dangerous and destructive weapons. Repent of wishing evil on others; it has created weapons against them. Repent of sending or firing evil weapons at others. In so doing, you will save yourself from being attacked by the weapons that you yourself created for another, but can ultimately come back at you and hit you.

Haven't you noticed that miserable, grumbling, unhappy people have miserable lives? What they keep wishing for on others keeps coming back to them. It is that simple. It could be a one-time wish, or a repetitive evil wish but all that stuff backfires eventually. Return to sender is built in, but especially if you pray it and say it.

Dear Reader

Thank you for acquiring and reading this book. Evil arrows are a real thing; they are flying around here all day and all night, looking for their targets.

Don't be a target.

Psalm 91 talks about all kinds of things walking and flying at night – evil arrows. The NT tells us that while we sleep the enemy is sowing tares --, might as well say, evil arrows.

How many people do you know who are baffled as to how they woke up like this, and not in a good way. They didn't go to bed sick, but they woke up ill.

May you increase in Knowledge and Wisdom and may the Lord put a hedge of protection around you to protect you from every fiery dart and arrow sent to you, your home, marriage, business, family, children, career, and health.

Do not lose heart if you get shot at. Joseph was shot at, but he persevered, and God turned all that was intended for his harm into good.

Joseph is a fruitful bough, even a fruitful bough by a well; whose branches run over the wall:

The archers have sorely grieved him, and shot at him, and hated him:

But his bow abode in strength, and the arms of his hands were made strong by the hands of the mighty God of Jacob; (from thence is the shepherd, the stone of Israel:)

Even by the God of thy father, who shall help thee; and by the Almighty, who shall bless thee with blessings of heaven above, blessings of the deep that lieth under, blessings of the breasts, and of the womb: (Genesis 49:22-25)

The Lord bless and keep you, in the Name of Jesus,

Amen.

Dr. Marlene Miles

References:

See *Repentance* prayers on this channel and also, soulish and diabolical Prayer treatment, Every Evil Arrow prayer, on this channel and also warfare prayer channel.

Recommended: *Repentance Prayer*, **Soulish & Diabolical Prayer Treatment**, message/book by this author. https://a.co/d/0NCqytH

Every Evil Arrow message/book by this author. https://a.co/d/1eFsL1B

Devil Weapons: Anger, Unforgiveness & Bitterness also by this author. https://a.co/d/dCPgsAH

Prayer books by this author

While most books by this author have prayer points either throughout the book or at the end, there are some books that are **only** prayers. You just open up the book and pray. They are listed below:

Prayers Against Barrenness: *For Success in Business and Life*

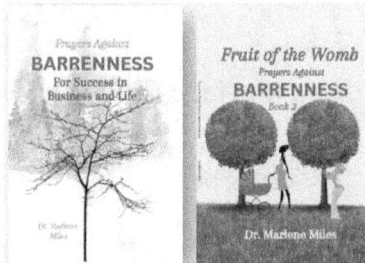

Fruit of the Womb: *Prayers Against Barrenness*

Beauty Curses, *Warfare Prayers Against*
https://a.co/d/5Xlc20M

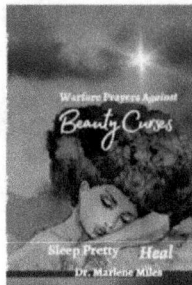

Courts of Marriage: Prayers for Marriage in the Courts of Heaven
(prayerbook) https://a.co/d/cNAdgAq

Courtroom Warfare @ Midnight
(prayerbook) https://a.co/d/5fc7Qdp

Demonic Cobwebs *(prayerbook)*
https://a.co/d/fp9Oa2H

Every Evil Bird https://a.co/d/hF1kh1O

Every Evil Arrow
https://a.co/d/afgRkiA

Gates of Thanksgiving

I Call Down Fire (new!)
https://a.co/d/hN7kGnE

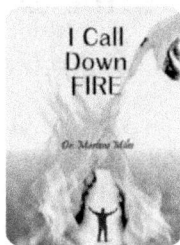

Spirits of Death & the Grave, Pass Over Me and My House
https://a.co/d/dS4ewyr

Please note that my name is spelled incorrectly on amazon, but not on the book.

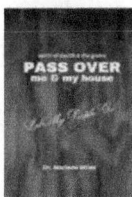

Throne of Grace: Courtroom Prayer

https://a.co/d/fNMxcM9

Warfare Prayer Against Poverty
https://a.co/d/bZ61lYu

Other books by this author

AK: *The Adventures of the Agape Kid*

AMONG SOME THIEVES

Ancestral Powers https://a.co/d/9prTyFf

Backstabbers https://a.co/d/gi8iBxf

Barrenness, *Prayers Against*
https://a.co/d/feUltIs

Battlefield of Marriage, *The*

Blindsided: *Has the Old Man Bewitched You?* https://a.co/d/5O2fLLR

Break Free from Collective Captivity

Casting Down Imaginations
https://a.co/d/1UxlLqa

Choose An Altar to Choose A Church

Churchzilla, The Wanna-Be, Supposed-to-be Bride of Christ

Curses of Blind Men

Demonic Cobwebs (prayerbook)

Demonic Time Bombs

Demons Hate Questions

Devil Loves Trauma, *The*

Devil Weapons: Unforgiveness, Bitterness,...

The Devourers: *Thieves of Darkness 2*

Do Not Swear by the Moon

Don't Refuse Me, Lord (4 book series)
https://a.co/d/idP34LG

Dream Defilement

The Emptiers: *Thieves of Darkness, 1*
https://a.co/d/5I4n5mc

Every Evil Arrow
https://a.co/d/afgRkiA

Evil Touch https://a.co/d/gSGGpS1

Failed Assignment
https://a.co/d/3CXtjZY

Fantasy Spirit Spouse
https://a.co/d/hW7oYbX

FAT Demons (The): *Breaking Demonic Curses*

The Fold (5-book series)

- The Fold (Book 1)
- Name Your Seed (Book 2)
- The Poor Attitudes of Money (3)
- Do Not Orphan Your Seed (4)
- For the Sake of the Gospel (5)
- My Sowing Journal

Gang Ups: Touch Not God's Anointed

got HEALING? Verses for Life

got LOVE? Verses for Life

got HOPE? Verses for Life

got money? https://a.co/d/g2av41N

How to Dental Assist

How to Dental Assist2: Be Productive, Not Wasteful

I Take It Back

It's Coming Back: Vengeance Is the Lord's, So Stop Making Weapons

Legacy

Let Me Have A Dollar's Worth
https://a.co/d/h8F8XgE

Level the Playing Field

Living for the NOW of God

Lose My Location
https://a.co/d/crD6mV9

Man Safari, *The*

Marriage Ed. Rules of Engagement & Marriage

Made Perfect in Love

Money Hunters: Beware of Those

Money on the Altar https://a.co/d/4EqJ2Nr

Mulberry Tree https://a.co/d/9nR9rRb

Motherboard (The) - *Soul Prosperity Series*

Name Your Seed

Occupy: *Until I Return*

Plantation Souls

Players Gonna Play

Power Money: Nine Times the Tithe

https://a.co/d/gRt41gy

The Power of Wealth *(forthcoming)*

Powers Above

The Robe, Part 1, The Lessons of Joseph

The Robe, Part II, The Lessons of Joseph

Seasons of Grief

Seasons of Waiting

Seasons of War

Second Marriage, Third--, *Any Marriage*

https://a.co/d/6m6GN4N

Sift You Like Wheat

Six Men Short: What Has Happened to all the Men?

Soul Prosperity soul prosperity series 3

https://a.co/d/5p8YvCN

Souls Captivity soul prosperity series 2

The Spirit of Poverty

StarStruck

SUNBLOCK

Upgrade: How to Get Out of Survival Mode

- Toxic Souls (Book 2 of series)
- Legacy (Book 3 of series)

The Wasters: *Thieves of Darkness,* Bk 2
https://a.co/d/bUvI9Jo

What Have You to Declare? What Do You Have With You from Where You've Been?

When I Was A Child, *I Prayed As a Child*

When the Devourer is Rebuked

https://a.co/d/1HVv8oq

The Wilderness Romance *(series)* This series is about conducting a Godly relationship and marriage with someone who is a Wilderness person. It is about how to recognize it and navigate through it. These books are about how not to get caught up in such.

- *The Social Wilderness*
- *The Sexual Wilderness*
  - *The Spiritual Wilderness*